ROCK PAINTING
For
Kids

PAINTING PROJECTS FOR ROCKS
OF ANY KIND YOU CAN FIND

Lin Wellford

FOR
YOUNG
READERS

for Skye, Erika, and Kira

Racehorse Publishing books may be purchased in bulk at special discounts for sales promotion, corporate gifts, fund-raising, or educational purposes. Special editions can also be created to specifications. For details, contact the Special Sales Department, Skyhorse Publishing, 307 West 36th Street, 11th Floor, New York, NY 10018 or info@skyhorsepublishing.com.

Racehorse Publishing™ and Racehorse for Young Readers™ are registered trademarks of Skyhorse Publishing, Inc.®, a Delaware corporation.

Visit our website at www.skyhorsepublishing.com.

10 9 8 7 6 5 4 3

Library of Congress Cataloging-in-Publication Data is available on file.

Cover Designer: Michael Short
Editor: Maggie Moschell
Interior Designer: Brian Roeth
Production Coordinator: Mark Griffin
Production Artist: Kath Bergstrom
Photographers: Lin Wellford and Christine Polomsky

Print ISBN: 978-1-63158-295-0
E-Book ISBN: 978-1-63158-297-4

Printed in China

Portions of the book were previously published
Painting on Rocks for Kids (978-1-58180-255-9)
by North Light Books in 2002.

About the Author

The author at age 10

Do you know the fairy tale about the person who learns to spin straw into gold? That's what it feels like to turn plain old rocks into art! When I was younger, I liked to draw and practiced so much that I became pretty good at it, but the first time I painted a rock, I knew that I had found something really special. It feels almost like magic to take a rock and change it into a little house, a bunch of flowers or a cuddly teddy bear.

I have always loved writing, so I am very happy to have found a career that allows me to do my two most favorite things.

As you try painting your own rocks, I hope you'll remember that part of the fun is seeing how much better your results will be with time and effort. Every rock can be a "stepping stone" that takes you farther along the path to becoming an artist yourself! So, keep rockin'!

Acknowledgments

Special thanks to Erin Robertson for helping to paint many of these projects as well as providing lots of inspiration and advice. Erin is proof that you can be a real artist at any age!

here are the projects you can do!

tips for painting rocks

Rocks are a great natural art material. They come in many different shapes and sizes. By adding details with paint, you can turn rocks into all kinds of amazing things. Pick up a rock and ask yourself what it looks like.

Not all rocks are good for painting. Some are too bumpy or rough, or they soak up paint like a sponge. Look for rocks that are smooth. Rocks that have been tumbled in water, such as in a river or creek, are the easiest to paint, but you can also use chunky rocks and pieces of fieldstone as long as the sides are not too rough. You can even paint pieces of broken concrete.

- Always scrub your rocks before you begin painting. Paint won't stick to a dirty rock.
- You'll need a paper plate, plastic lid or plastic artist's palette for mixing your paint.
- Never let paint dry on your brushes. It turns them all stiff and yucky.

- Always rinse your brush between colors. Have paper towels handy for wiping your brush.
- Pour paint in little puddles, about the size of your thumbnail. Big puddles dry up before you can use them.
- Wear old clothes and push up your sleeves when you paint. If you get acrylic paint on your clothes, scrub it off with an old toothbrush, soap and plenty of water before it dries. Dried acrylic paint may never come out of fabric.
- Spread newspaper over your work area. You can wipe your brush and make test strokes on it. Also it will slow down a spill if you tip over your water.

And the most important thing to remember is
- You can't ruin a rock! If you make a mistake, just wipe off the paint before it dries, or let it dry and then paint over it.

A clean paintbrush

is a happy paintbrush.

Remember to rinse your brush

after each color.

Paint

tempera paint

For the projects in this book, you'll need a set of basic colors of acrylic paint. You can also decorate rocks with tempera paint, watercolors, paint pens, markers, gel pens, colored pencils, or nail polish.

acrylic paint

If your painted rocks will be just for decoration indoors, the kind of paint you use doesn't matter. If your rocks are going to be used outside or soaked in water, you should use outdoor acrylic paint, which is found at most craft stores. It stays on the rocks better than regular acrylic paint.

outdoor acrylic paint

Paintbrushes

You will need just three brushes:
- a wide flat brush like the two brushes on the far right
- a medium brush like the two in the middle
- a small, skinny brush like the green one

Other helpful things
- Cotton swabs for blending
- Pencil, marker, or white pencil for drawing the designs on the rocks
- Air-dry clay for rocks that tip over
- Dimensional paint for puffy lines or dots
- Acrylic floor wax for making the rocks shiny

brushes, paint, and more

watercolors

markers

colored pencils

all about rocks

Where to find rocks

You may find good rocks near creeks, streams, beaches, and lakes. In some areas rocks seem to be lying around every- where, and in other places it may take a lot of hunting to find them. Don't take rocks out of the water in places where they may be homes for crayfish or other animals. State and national parks do not allow visitors to take any- thing home, including rocks. It's a good idea to ask for permission before you gather rocks outside your own yard.

You can buy rocks of all sizes from landscaping companies or gardening stores. Once you start looking for rocks, you'll be amazed at the unexpected places you'll find them.

Small rocks are fun, too!

Most of the rocks in this book fit into the palm of your hand. If you can't find many rocks this size, don't worry; there are still lots of things you can do with smaller rocks. Here are just a few ideas:

Make Faces
Use flat pebbles to create silly face rocks.

Put 'em Together
Use white glue and pebbles or gravel to make pictures, names, or designs. Colored aquarium gravel is sold at pet stores. Make sure to allow plenty of drying time when you glue rocks.

8

Message Rocks
Do you have something to
say? Write it on stone!

Name Game
Amaze your
friends with spe-
cial rocks painted
just for them!
These make great
party favors, too.

Clever Constructions
Even the tiniest pebbles can
be glued together with white
glue to create all kinds of fun
stuff. Use crumpled foil to
hold the pebbles in place
while the glue dries. Wait
until the next day to start
painting them.

go fish!

66 I wanted a pet fish, but Mom said I had to wait until I was old enough to remember to feed it. At the creek I saw a rock that gave me an idea. Why not make a rock fish? A rock fish doesn't mind if I never feed him! Here's how I made mine. 99

Make a Fishbowl
Put gravel or marbles in the bottom of a fishbowl and add water, a plastic plant, and your painted fish (painted with outdoor acrylic paint). Prop up your fish with a smaller rock. Paint other rocks to add to the scene.

1

Find a fish-shaped rock

Choose a smooth, flat rock that has a "fishy" shape. Pictures of real fish can give you ideas. When you find a rock you like, scrub it clean.

2

Draw the fish

Use a pencil to draw the head with a curved line and give the fish a round eye. At the other end, draw a fan-shaped tail and draw triangles above and below the tail.

You can use these fish as guides for drawing your fish. Or you can enlarge them on a copier and trace one onto your rock with carbon paper.

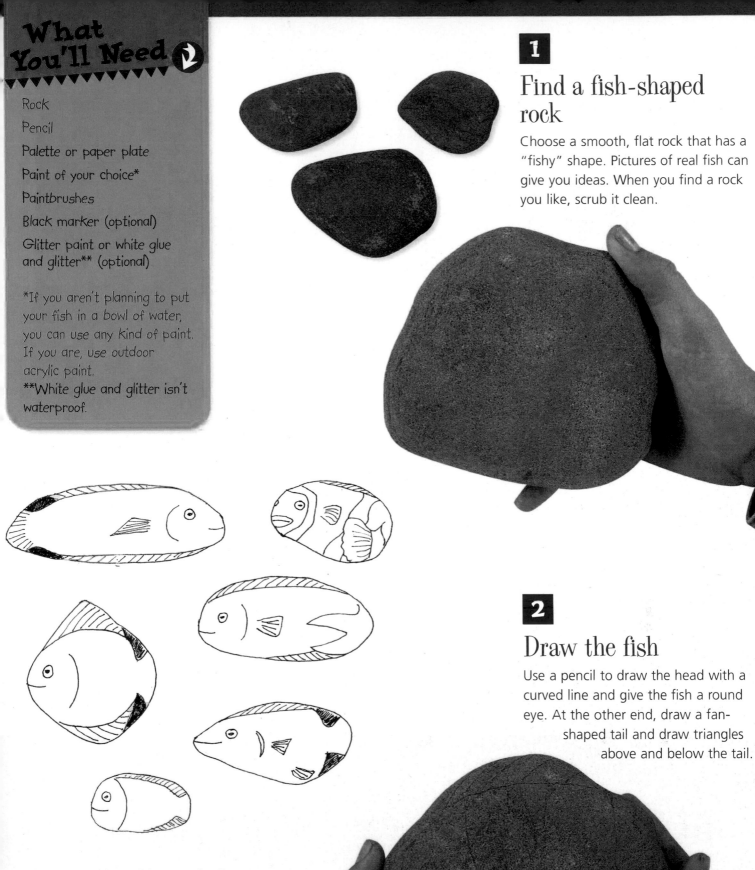

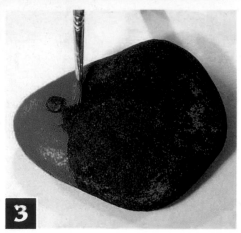

3
Paint the head
Use a bright color and your large brush to paint the fish's head. Paint all the way around the edges so no plain rock shows, but leave the circle for the eye unpainted.

4
Paint around the tail
Use black paint and your medium brush to fill in the triangles above and below the tail. The black paint makes those parts seem to disappear.

5
Outline the eye
Make a black outline around the eye with a black marker or your skinny brush, keeping the outside edge round and neat. The inside edge will get covered up later.

Remember to rinse your brush

after each color.

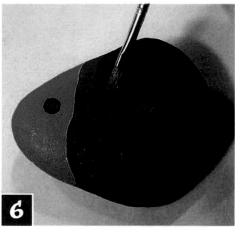

6
Paint the body
Pick a color for the body. Mix three drops of this color with one drop of white, and paint the fish's body.

7
Paint the tail
Mix three drops of white and one drop of the body color for the tail. Save this puddle of paint for step 9.

TIPS FOR PAINTING GOOD LINES
1. Thin the paint with a little water.
2. Hold your brush handle straight up.
3. Paint with just the tip of the brush.
4. Paint lines with one smooth stroke, not a lot of little sketchy lines.
5. If you mess up, wipe the line off with a damp paper towel and try again.
6. The more you practice, the better you'll get!

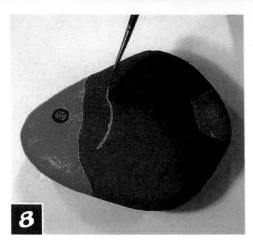

8
Paint the gill
When the paint on the body is dry, use your skinny brush to add a light-colored curved gill line just behind the head. I used yellow.

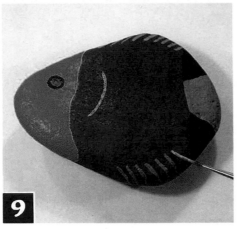

9
Paint fins
Clean the skinny brush, and dip it in the tail color to paint short, slanted lines for the top and bottom fins.

10
Paint the eye and lip
Use your skinny brush with red paint to fill in the middle of the eye. Then make a red line for the mouth. Rinse the brush, and use black paint to paint a pupil in the eye.

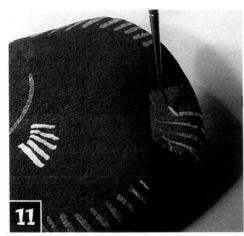

11
Add white lines
Use your skinny brush to make a small fan-shaped fin behind and below the gill line. Also add some lines to the tail, curving them out at the top and bottom to fit the fin shape.

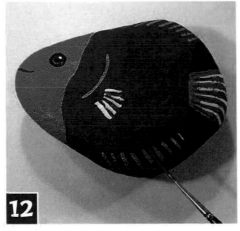

12
Dot the eye
Last, add a tiny dot of white off center in your fish's eye. For extra decoration, I painted little purple lines between all the fin and tail lines.

13
Add finishing touches
If you want, you can paint your fish with glitter paint or (if you won't be putting your fish in water) white glue sprinkled with glitter. I also added dots of paint to the body.

13

rocky roadsters

66 I made a race-track in my sandbox and I needed some cars to put on the roads. My brother said sand would jam up the wheels of toy cars, so I decided to make "rockmobiles" instead. This is how I made them. 99

1

Pick a car-shaped rock

Rocks with flat bottoms and rounded tops make good cars. Rocks with square corners can be trucks. You might even find a rock shaped like a roadster with a long hood. Wash your rock and scrub away any slimy stuff.

2

Draw the car

Follow the steps above to draw a car on your rock. Use a pencil so you can erase any mistakes.

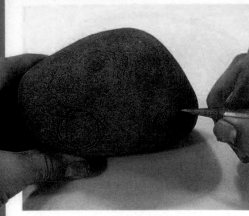

Here's how I drew the car on my rock.

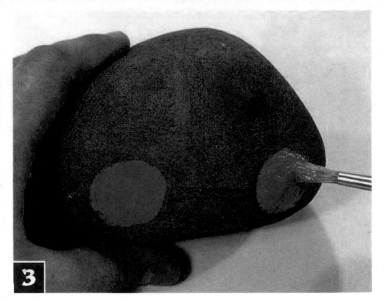

3

Paint the tires

Mix two drops of white with one drop of black to make gray. Use your small brush to fill in all the wheel circles. All four wheels should be the same size and as round as you can make them.

> **PAINTING TIP**
>
> For better results, pull your brush across the rock in smooth strokes instead of dabbing on the paint.

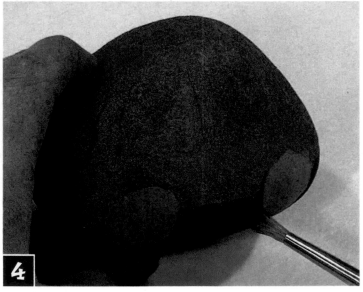

4

Make part of the rock "disappear"

It's almost magical the way painting an area black makes that part of the rock seem to vanish. Use black paint to fill in the space around the bottoms of the wheels and below the car body on both sides and each end.

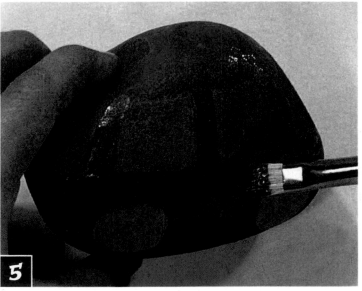

5

Paint the car body

Pick a color for your car. Dark colors cover in one coat, but a light color may need two coats. Use your medium brush to paint the sides and ends. Then paint the top. Let the paint dry before going to the next step.

Paint the windows

Paint the windows black. Use the skinny brush to paint around the edges, making them as smooth and straight as you can. Then use a bigger brush to fill in the centers.

Paint the wheel hubs

While you still have black paint on your skinny brush, make a big circle in the center of each wheel and fill it in with solid black. Make all these wheel hubs the same size.

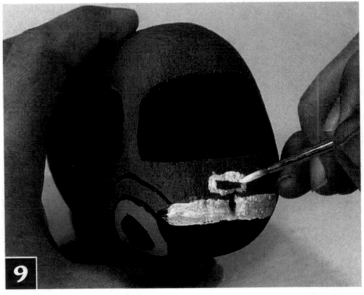

Paint the fenders

Use a black marker or your skinny brush with black paint thinned with a little water to paint the curved fenders above each wheel. Connect the front and back fenders with a straight line. Paint two lines for the door (see step 10 for a picture of the door).

Paint the bumpers

Clean your brush. Between the fenders, use white to paint bumpers with rounded corners. Paint a license plate on the back bumper. After the paint dries, use the skinny brush or a marker to paint letters or numbers on the license plate.

10

Paint wheel spokes

Use your skinny brush to paint a white circle inside each black hub circle. Paint an X in the middle, then paint a line sideways and one up and down.

11

Paint the door handles

Then use the same brush to paint white curved lines for the door handles.

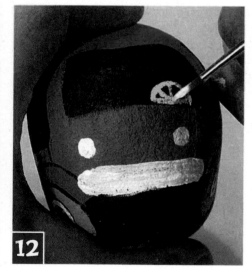

12

Paint the steering wheel

Use the same brush to paint a white steering wheel on the driver's side of the front windshield. Paint round white headlights and smaller taillights. Painting white first will make the red and yellow paint show up better.

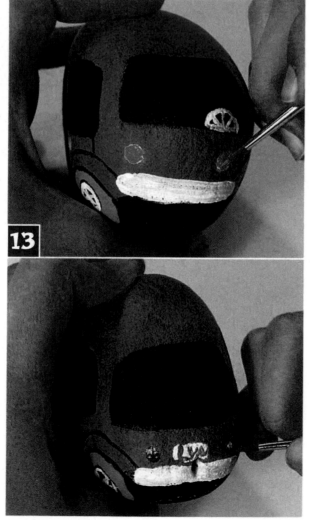

13

Paint headlights and taillights

When the white is dry, use red paint for the taillights and bright yellow paint for the headlights. You can add sparkle with glitter paint if you want. For a shiny car, paint it with clear acrylic floor wax.

more ideas

SCHOOL BUS

19

lazy lizards

> A big green lizard was sunning himself on a rock in our garden. When I tried to catch him, he scurried away, so I took the rock inside and painted my own lizard on it. This lizard never runs away from me! Here is how I did it.

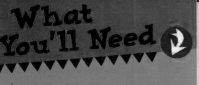
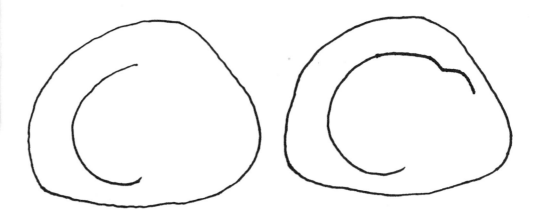

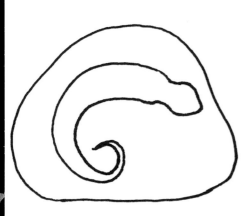

Follow these steps to draw a lizard

1

Choose a rock and draw the lizard

Your rock should be smooth and have enough room in the middle to fit a lizard's curved body and tail. Scrub the rock and draw the lizard on it. Trace this lizard and enlarge it on a copy machine or draw your own lizard following the steps shown above.

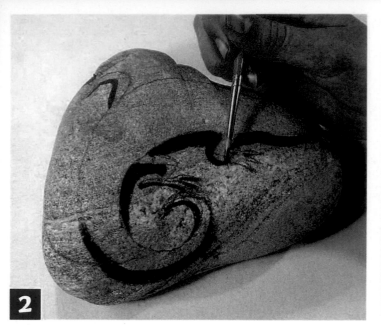

2

Make shadows

Use black paint and your small brush to paint thick black shadows around part of the lizard. Make the shadows below the legs thinner.

3

Paint the lizard yellow

Rinse your brush and paint the lizard yellow to make the final coat of paint look brighter. Use a small brush to outline the lizard and to fill in the toes and the tip of the tail. Then use a bigger brush to fill in the rest.

4

Paint the body

I painted my lizard green, but yours can be any color you like. Use your medium brush to paint the top of the lizard's body, leaving an oval-shaped area for the eye. Also leave his tummy and parts of the tail and legs yellow. Use your skinny brush for the toes, tip of the tail, and under the eye.

5

Add stripes

Mix a darker color (I mixed blue and green). Use your small brush to paint a line along the top edge of the yellow tummy, the legs, tail, and top of the body.

PAINTING TIP

A long line should be painted in one long, smooth stroke instead of lots of small sketchy lines.

Add rows of spots

Use the same color to make two rows of dots from the neck to the end of the tail, making the dots smaller as you go. Make them big enough so you can paint yellow spots on top.

Fill in the eye

Rinse your brush and use black paint to paint a small oval eye in the center of the yellow eye area. Give the eye pointed ends like a little football. Also make two tiny black dots for nostrils at the end of the nose.

Paint white highlights

Use your small brush to add a line of white along the bottom edge of the lizard to help the yellow tummy stand out. Paint white on the neck, under the chin, and around the eye. Make a tiny white dot in the eye.

Add finishing touches

Use a small brush or dimensional paint to paint a yellow dot on the top edge of each blue-green spot so that a little of the darker color shows.

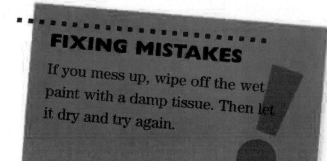

FIXING MISTAKES

If you mess up, wipe off the wet paint with a damp tissue. Then let it dry and try again.

Lizards and salamanders can be painted in a rainbow of colors. Paint a whole collection to decorate your rock garden or fill a terrarium.

4

flower power

66 My grand-mother's birthday was coming, and I wanted to make something special for her. She really likes flowers, so I thought; "Why not paint a flower rock for her?" She loves it! Here's how I did it. 99

What You'll Need

Large rock
Pencil
White colored pencil
Palette or paper plate
Paint of your choice
Paintbrushes
Clear acrylic spray (optional)

1

Choose a rock

Lots of rock sizes and shapes make good flower rocks. You can use round rocks or chunky rocks that will stand up on one flat end. Whatever the shape, rocks that have mostly smooth surfaces are the easiest to paint. When you have your rock, scrub it and let it dry.

2

Divide your rock

Use a pencil to make a line around the bottom third of your rock. Keep this line as level as possible all the way around or your flower bowl will look uneven.

Remember to rinse your brush

after each color.

3

Paint the bowl

Pick a color for the bowl. I chose blue to match my grandmother's sofa. Add two drops of white to this color. Use your biggest brush to paint the bowl all the way down to the bottom. Let the paint dry.

Paint the background

Rinse your brush and mix green with enough black to make a very dark green. A dark color behind the leaves and flowers will make them stand out. Paint this color from the top down to the bowl. Let the paint dry.

Draw the leaves

Use a white pencil to draw different-size oval leaves. Start with a cluster at the top, then work down. Overlap the leaves and draw a few that hang over the edge of the bowl. It's OK to have irregular spaces between the leaves.

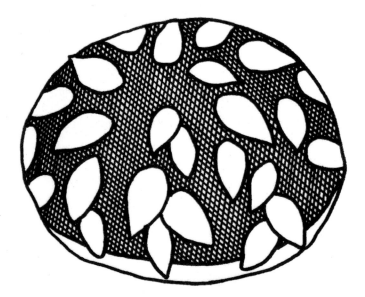

Your leaves should look something like this.

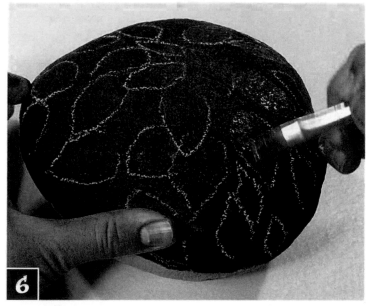

Paint some of the leaves

Use a small or medium brush and green paint to paint all the leaves at the very top of your rock. Then use this same color to paint other leaves here and there.

Paint light green leaves

Rinse your brush and mix equal amounts of yellow and green to make light green. Use this to paint more leaves, again skipping around.

Paint the rest of the leaves

Finally, add a little more green to the light green mixture to make an in-between color and paint the rest of the leaves.

Detail the leaves

Mix a little black with green to make dark green. Use a skinny brush to add a crease down the center of all the dark green leaves. Use plain green to paint the creases in the other leaves. Use black paint to outline the places where the leaves overlap.

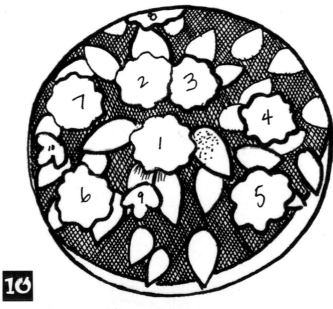

Draw flower shapes

When the paint is dry, use a white pencil to draw three flowers in the center (numbers 1, 2, and 3 above). Add others around the edges (4 to 8). Numbers 9 and 10 are buds. Draw some flowers close together and others farther apart.

Paint white flowers

Use your medium brush and white paint to fill in all the flower shapes. Let it dry and paint a second coat if needed.

Add petal details

An easy way to paint flowers is to paint a curl in the middle of each flower with a small brush and red paint. Begin in the center each time. The spirals will look better if they are a little uneven or if there are small gaps in the lines.

Add flower buds

Fill in any plain-looking places with a few flower buds. Mix pale pink by adding a touch of red to a drop of white. Use your medium brush to make a center oval shape and add two smaller ovals, one on each side.

Paint bud details

Use your small brush with red paint to outline the inside edges of the two side ovals, and one straight line up the center. Rinse the brush and use the dark green from step 9 to paint a cluster of lines on the top of the bud.

more ideas

If you want to make your rock shiny, ask an adult to please spray it with clear acrylic spray, which also protects the paint. If you used outdoor acrylic paint, your flower rocks can be displayed outside.

There are lots of ways to paint flowers on rocks.

You can paint flowers on a rock that is too uneven to stand on its own. "Plant" it in a flowerpot!

PROJECT 5
rockosaurs

" What would it *be* like to have a dinosaur for a pet? I guess I'd need a bigger room! I painted some dinosaurs on rocks and took them to school when we were studying prehistoric reptiles. Everyone thought they were cool. "

2

Paint a basecoat

A coat of yellow paint will make the final paint color look brighter, especially on dark-colored rocks. Use your large brush to paint the whole rock, except for the very bottom. Let the paint dry before you go on. Clean your brush.

1

Choose a rock

Rocks with flat bottoms and curving tops work best. Scrub your rock clean. If the bottom of your rock is not level, add air-dry clay to the wet rock as shown on page 45. Let the clay dry overnight before painting your rock.

3

Paint the rock orange

Paint the rock orange, which is red mixed with yellow, or choose another color. Let it dry.

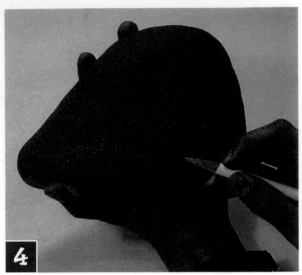

On the front of your rock, draw an oval about the size of your thumbprint. Add neck lines to the head, curving them down and around the corner of the rock, but leaving room below the bottom neck line for the front legs.

Draw the dinosaur

Follow the drawings to draw a dinosaur on your rock.

Draw the tail so the tip points to the neck. Draw the front leg, then a tummy line from behind the front leg to the tail.

Make a big oval haunch that curves above the top of the tail. Draw a back foot where the tail curves up from the bottom of the rock.

Turn your rock around and draw the other front leg. Draw another oval haunch and back leg plus a tummy line between the two legs.

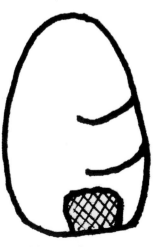

Here is the way your rock should look from the front edge.

Paint the open spaces

Use a medium or large brush with black paint to darken the spaces around the legs and below the body.

Paint black on the back

Also darken the spaces between the two front legs and around the legs on the back of the rock.

Add shading

Add enough water to some brown paint so you can see through it. Use a cotton swab or paintbrush to add brown shadows below the head and neck, around the haunch, and under the tail. Before the paint dries, soften the edges of the shadows by rubbing them with a dry paintbrush.

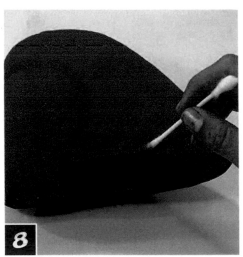

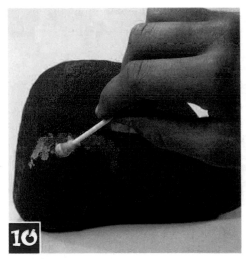

Add shading to the back

Add shadows to the back of your dinosaur around the haunch and on the bottom of the tummy.

Paint highlights

Mix two drops of yellow with one drop of white. Use a damp cotton swab or medium stiff brush to scrub this color along the top half of the head and neck, the top of the haunch, and the top of the tail. Soften the edges with a dry paintbrush.

Repeat

Paint highlights along the top edge of the haunch on the back side, too.

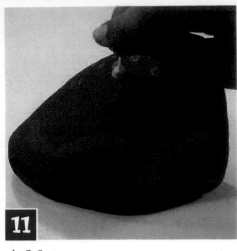

11

Add spots

Use the same cotton swab (or a small brush) and yellow paint to add clusters of spots to the top of the dinosaur.

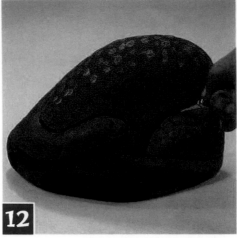

12

Add black details

Use your small brush and black paint (or a black marker) to make a tiny dot for a nostril, a curved mouth line, and a round eye. Then outline the head, neck, haunches, and tail with black paint to make them stand out.

13

Add yellow details

Rinse your brush and make light outlines along the tummy, the tail, and the neck with the yellow paint from step 9. Add a row of short, curved lines to the bottom edge of the tail and longer curved lines on the tummy. Turn the rock over and paint tummy lines on the back of the dinosaur.

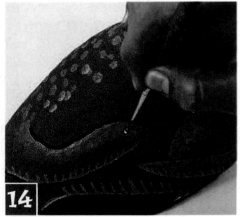

14

Add white touches

Use your small brush and white paint to make a tiny C shape inside the black eye circle. If you mess up, let the paint dry, then fix it with black paint. Paint a white dot in the eye. Add three half-circle toenails to each foot.

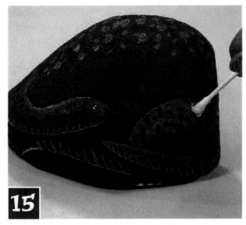

15

Create more texture

Pick up a little red paint with a clean, damp cotton swab or your small brush to add more dots to the dinosaur's back and the tops of the haunches. Add smaller dots to the yellow places on the neck and tail.

Look at your rock from every angle to make sure it looks finished.

more ideas

There are lots of other kinds of dinosaurs that you can paint on rocks. You could even try turning a dinosaur into a dragon!

35

PROJECT 6

go buggy!

❝ When I told my friends I was going to give them cooties, you should have seen the faces they made! Now everyone wants me to "bug" them! Here is how I painted my cootie bugs. ❞

1 Pick a rock

Any size smooth, round, or oval rock will work, but tiny rocks may be harder to paint. Scrub it clean.

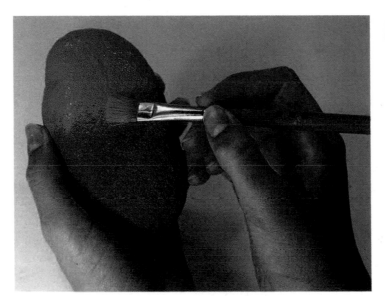

2 Paint a basecoat

Use a big flat brush to paint the top and sides of your rock with a light color of paint. You can leave the bottom unpainted. Let the paint dry.

3 Sketch the design

Use a white pencil to draw the bug. Make a line for the head, and add three curved lines for stripes. You may use a regular pencil, but draw the lines lightly so they won't show through the paint.

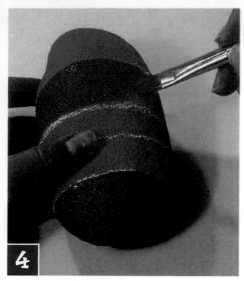

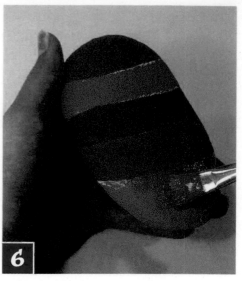

Paint the head and one stripe

Pick a different color and use your large brush to paint the head, making the edges neat and round. Then paint the third stripe this color.

Paint another stripe

Rinse your brush. When the paint is dry, paint the second stripe with bright red or a different color of your choice.

Paint the last stripe

Rinse your brush, then choose another color to paint the back end of the bug, covering the basecoat to the very bottom edges of the rock. I used a mixture of yellow and green.

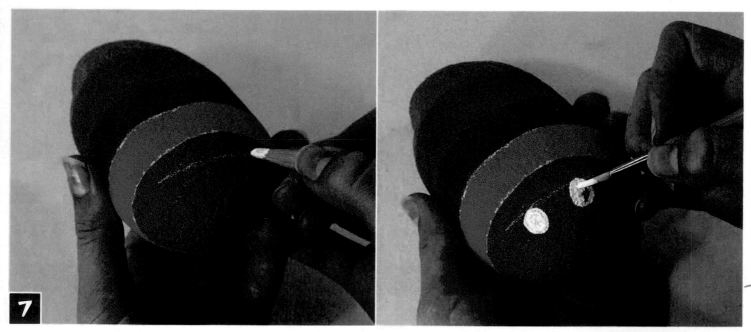

Draw and paint the eyes

To keep the eyes level, sketch a straight line across the top part of the head and draw two round eyes that are the same size. Use your small brush and white paint to fill in the eye circles.

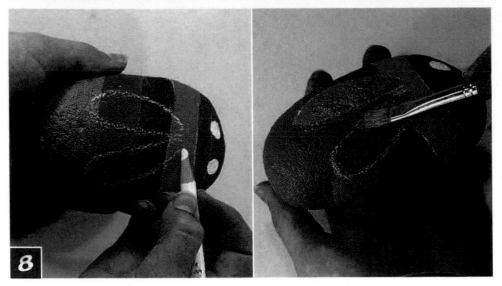

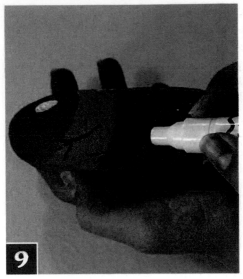

Draw and paint the wings

When the stripes are dry, draw two long oval wings that come to points at the center of the first stripe. Use a large or medium brush and a new color of paint to fill in these wing shapes. I used purple.

Add legs and feet

Use your small brush and black paint (or a black marker) to draw three curved legs on each side of its body. Draw the feet any shape you wish.

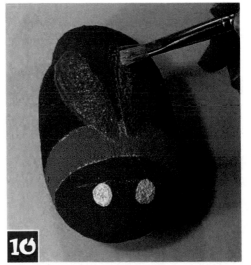

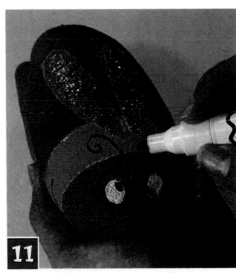

Add glitter if you want

I added glitter paint to the wings, but you may want to put glitter on one of the stripes instead. Use your imagination to make your bug special.

Add details

Use a black marker or a small brush and black paint to give your bug a wiggly mouth line, two goofy-looking eyeballs, and a pair of curly feelers.

Remember to rinse your brush

after each color.

more ideas

There are lots of different bugs you can paint, from ones that look real to some that are really silly.

PROJECT 7
sandbox city

66 My rock cars gave me the idea to make a city to go with them. I looked around and found lots of rocks shaped like all kinds of buildings. They were fun to paint, too. Here's how you can make a really easy rock house. 99

What You'll Need ↻

Rock

Pencil

Palette or paper plate

Paint of your choice

Paintbrushes

Cotton swab (optional)

Black marker (optional)

1

Pick a rock

Rocks for buildings should have flat bottoms and flat fronts. Rocks with square tops make good stores. Houses should have slanted or pointed tops. Scrub the rock clean.

2

Draw the design

Use a pencil to sketch the door in the center of the rock. Draw square or rectangular windows on each side of the door so that the tops line up. Make a third window near the top. Draw two straight lines along the front, sides and the back for the roof. If your rock is thick enough, add windows to the sides of the rock.

Paint the walls

Your house may be any color you like. I mixed black and white to make gray. Use a large or medium brush to paint the front, sides, and back of your house, leaving the doors, windows, and roof unpainted.

Paint the roof

Rinse your brush and paint the roof, but not the area under it, which is called the eaves. I painted my roof black. Other good color combinations are white walls with a dark green roof, light blue walls with a navy blue roof, yellow walls with a brown roof, and red walls with a white roof.

Paint the windows

Yellow windows make your house look cheerful and cozy. If your walls are yellow, paint the windows orange or a dark color. Use your small brush, and make the edges of the windows as straight as you can.

Add a glow

Mix a tiny amount of orange (red plus yellow). Use the tip of your finger, a damp cotton swab, or a small, dry brush to rub this color on the bottom part of each window.

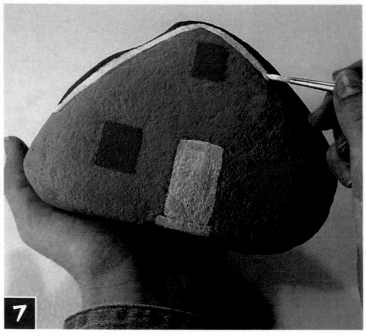

Paint the door and eaves

Use a small or medium brush and white paint to neatly fill in the shape of the door, keeping the edges smooth and straight. If there is room, add a doorstep below the door. Paint a white line under the roof for the eaves.

Add black outlines

Use black paint and the skinny brush or a black marker to outline the door, the doorstep, and the windows. Make a cross in each window. Straight lines in the corners help make the house look square. Add a doorknob.

Paint some bushes

Rinse your brush and mix green with a small amount of black to make dark green. Use this paint and your small brush to make pointed oval bushes on each side of the door and at the two corners of the house.

Paint flowers

Rinse your brush and switch to plain green to paint flower stems under each window. Keep them shorter than the bushes. Let these lines dry and rinse your brush before adding red flowers to the tops and middles of the stems.

Paint flowers on the bushes

Use the very tip of your skinniest brush to add dots for tiny flowers all over the bushes. I used purple. Now your rock house is finished!

more ideas

TOY STORE

GAS STATION

SWEET SHOP

There are lots of other kinds of rock buildings you can paint to add to your sandbox city. Look at the buildings in your neighborhood for ideas.

how to fix a wobbly rock!

What do you do with a rock that won't stand up? Add some air-dry clay to the bottom. The place where the clay was added won't show once the rock has been painted. This air-dry clay is sold at craft stores, but you can use any kind of clay that hardens without baking.

1 Scrub the rock clean. Clay sticks best to a wet rock.

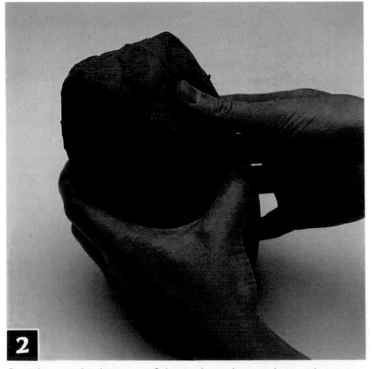

2 Put clay on the bottom of the rock and smooth it with your fingers. There shouldn't be any bumps where the clay and the rock meet.

3 Stand the rock on a table so the bottom of the clay becomes flat. If the rock still tips over, add more clay until the rock stands up. Leave the rock alone for 24 hours until the clay is dry.

45

playful food

" Did you ever pretend to run a restaurant? You can paint rocks to look like lots of different kinds of food. I made hamburgers for my picnic table restaurant. My dad thought they looked so good that he bought one to use as a paperweight on his desk. Here's how I made them. "

What You'll Need ↷

Rock

Pencil

White colored pencil

Palette or paper plate

Paint of your choice

Paintbrushes

White dimensional paint (optional)

Draw the bun lines

Draw a line all around the rock, a little bit above the center. Make another line below the first line, leaving enough space for the burger patty and toppings.

Paint the meat

Use your large or medium brush and brown paint to paint the meat, keeping the top and bottom edges as smooth and level as you can. Let the paint dry.

Find a hamburger-shaped rock

Look for round rocks that are flat on the bottom and rounded on top. They can be as big or small as you wish, but a rock that fits into your hand is perfect. Scrub the rock clean and let it dry.

4
Mix paint for the bun

Use your large brush to mix two drops of yellow, one drop of white, and one and a half drops of orange. Put a small drop of brown on your palette and pick up a little on the tip of your brush. Add it to the mix. Add touches of brown and white until the mixture is the color of a bun.

5
Paint the bun

Use your large brush to cover the entire top half of the bun with the bun color. When you are finished, don't rinse your brush, but use it to mix the next color.

Prop up your rock with a brush or a pencil when you paint the bottom bun. Let the paint dry before going on.

6
Paint a tan ring and the bottom bun

The bun should be lighter just above the meat. Mix a drop or two of white paint with the paint left on your brush to make tan. Paint a narrow ring just above the meat. Use a dry brush to soften the edge where the two colors meet. Paint the bottom bun this tan color, too.

Remember to rinse your brush

after each color.

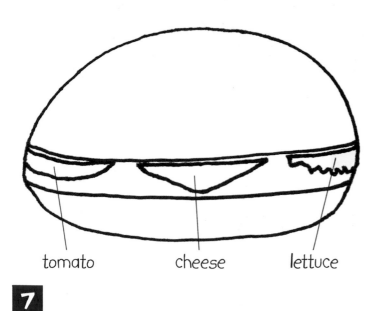

tomato   cheese   lettuce

7
Add the fillings

Use a white pencil to sketch four cheese triangles equally spaced around your meat. In the upper half of the meat, sketch a half-round tomato slice between the first two triangles, a ruffled edge of lettuce leaf between the next two, then another tomato slice, and a final lettuce leaf.

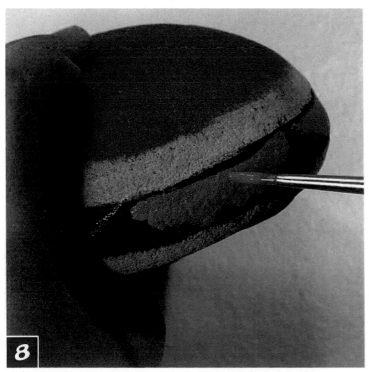

8
Paint a basecoat for the fillings

To help the fillings stand out, use your medium brush with yellow to paint all the shapes you just sketched. Leave a narrow ring of brown paint showing along the tops of the fillings. Make sure the edge of the lettuce looks wavy.

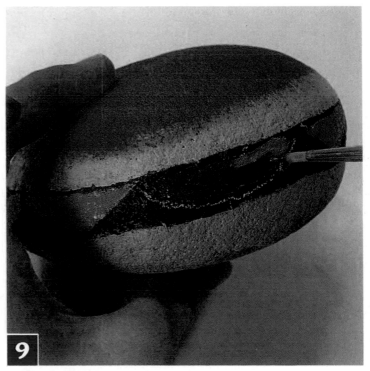

9
Paint the cheese and tomato

Rinse your brush. Then mix a tiny amount of red into a small drop of yellow to make a cheese color. Paint all four cheese triangles with this color. Rinse your brush and use red paint to paint the two tomato slices.

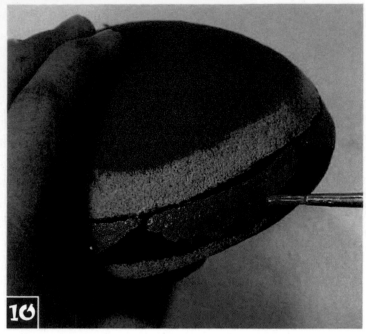

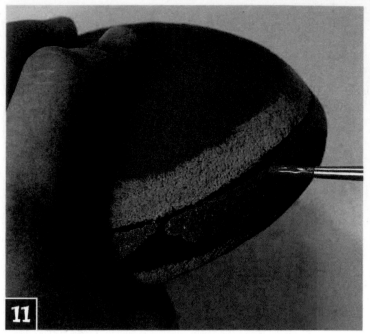

Paint the lettuce

Rinse your brush. Squeeze out a drop of yellow paint and add a little white and green to make a pale green color. Paint the two lettuce leaves, leaving a line of brown just above them.

Detail the lettuce

Add more green to the lettuce color and use this darker shade to paint short lines on the lettuce so it looks ruffled.

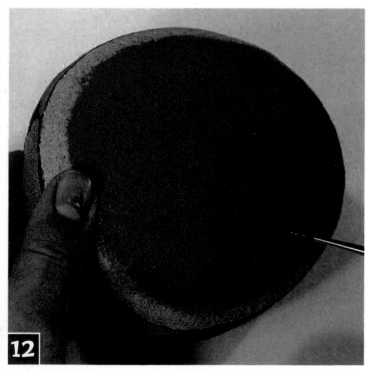

Dot the top of the bun

Use your smallest brush and brown paint to paint small dark dots over the top of the bun. (I made about fifty!) Don't put any around the sides.

Add sesame seeds

You can paint the seeds with white paint, or you can make real-looking seeds with white dimensional paint. Touch the tip of the bottle just off center of each brown spot, then lift up sideways. A rim of brown should show on one side. If you mess up, use a damp cotton swab to pick up the paint. When all the seeds are painted, let it dry for an hour.

50

more ideas

....

playful food

Try painting some pickle chips and sliced tomatoes to serve with your "burgers."

If you use your imagination when looking for food-shaped rocks, there is no telling what you'll find: sandwiches, cookies, fruit, or slices of pie, or pizza, to name just a few!

51

mystery eggs

" What if you discovered a strange-looking egg just as it was starting to hatch? What kind of creature would be inside? A dragon? A dinosaur? An alien? Maybe even a monster? Paint one and maybe you'll find out! "

1

Choose an egg-shaped rock

Any of these rocks would make a good egg. Look for an oval rock that is shaped like an egg. It can be any size, but one that is about as big as your fist makes a good first egg. Scrub it clean and let it dry.

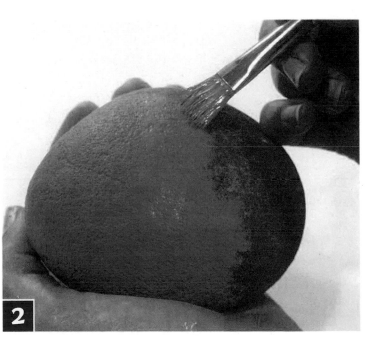

2

Paint the basecoat

Use your large brush to mix two big drops of white with one big drop of black. Paint your entire rock with this gray color. Let it dry before going to the next step.

3

Tear a sponge

Tear a small piece from a kitchen sponge so that it has ragged edges. Wet it and squeeze most of the water out.

Sponge on purple paint

Use a brush to spread a small puddle of purple paint (red mixed with blue) on your palette. Lightly press the damp sponge piece into the paint. Dab the sponge on a piece of newspaper, then pat it on your painted rock, turning it in different directions. You may have to do this several times. Let the paint dry.

Sponge on blue paint

Pour out a small puddle of blue paint. Rinse your sponge and squeeze it almost dry. Sponge blue paint on your rock just as you did in step 4. Let the paint dry. Rinse your sponge clean.

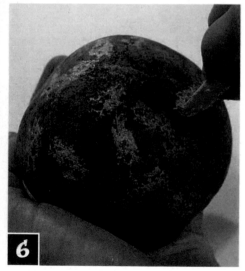

Sponge on silver paint

Now sponge on a coat of silver acrylic paint. If you don't have silver paint, use light gray. Sponge this color lightly so that the other colors show through. Let the paint dry.

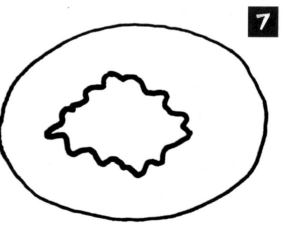

7 Outline the opening

Sketch a diamond-shaped opening on your rock, using the drawing at left as a guide. Use your small brush and black paint to outline the shape of the jagged hole. Wiggle your brush as you paint to make wavy lines.

Paint the center

Switch to your large brush to fill in the center of the shape with solid black.

Create large cracks

Use your smallest brush and black paint to paint large cracks around the outside of the opening. Make some thick and some thin, some short and some longer so that they don't look too much alike.

Remember
to rinse
your brush

after
each color.

Make tiny cracks

To make the smaller cracks, you can use a fine-tip black marker or a paint pen. Or mix a little water with some black paint and use the tip of your small brush to paint thin crooked lines that fan out from the ends of the cracks, some with two lines, some with more.

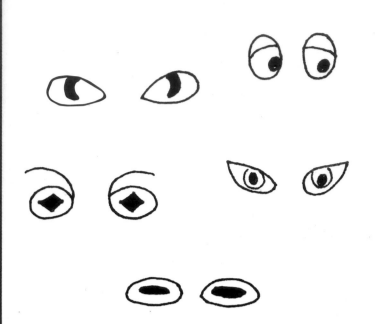

Paint the eyes

When the black paint is dry, use your small brush and white paint to paint two small eyes that are the same size. The eyes can be any shape you like. It may help to sketch them first with a white pencil. Let the paint dry.

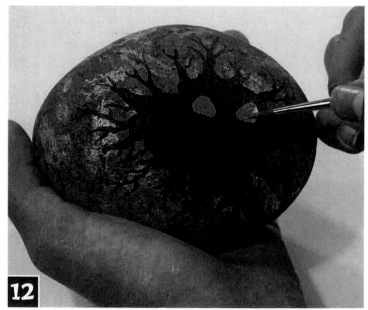

Paint the eye color

Mix lime green from yellow with just a touch of blue, or use glow-in-the-dark paint for a spooky effect. Use your small brush to paint this color over the white eye shapes.

Paint the pupils

Clean your small brush, then use black paint or a black marker to add two pupils. I made mine narrow and curved like cats' eyes. The pupils you paint may be different.

more ideas

Eggs can be painted in lots of different color combinations. Try adding the hint of a face with a long, forked tongue, or a scaly tail slipping out and perhaps a little claw showing, too.

bookend bears

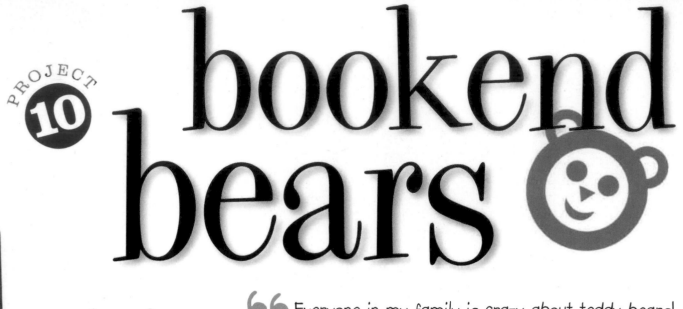

❝ Everyone in my family is crazy about teddy bears! I found an easy way to paint them on rocks. They make great bookends, but you can also use them as doorstops, paperweights, or decorations for your room. ❞

1

Find a bear-shaped rock

Look for tall rocks with flat bottoms. They can have a slight tilt to them. Medium-size ones are easiest to paint. Scrub the rock clean. If your rock won't stand up, add air-dry clay to the bottom as shown on page 45. Let the clay dry overnight before painting your rock.

2

Paint your rock

Use your large brush to paint the entire rock the color you've chosen for your bear. If your rock is dark, you may need to add a second coat. Let the paint dry.

3

Sketch the bear

Use a pencil to draw the bear on your rock, following the drawings on the next page.

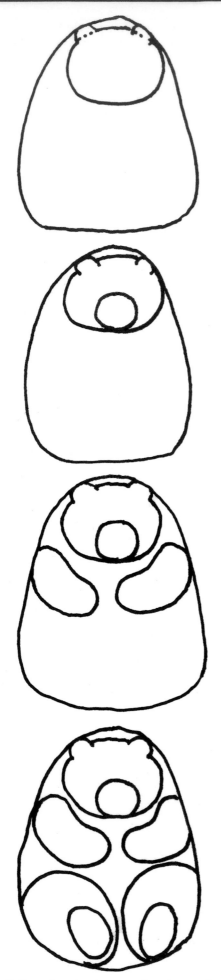

4

Paint dark outlines

Use dark paint and a small brush or a marker to paint over the pencil lines. Use brown paint if your bear is yellow or tan. If your bear is a different color, use a darker shade of the body color.

5

Paint fuzzy shadows

Dabbing in shadows with a brush or cotton swab will make your bear look fuzzy. Dip your small brush or swab in the dark paint from step 4 and dab it on newspaper first. Then dab the paint in the middle of the tummy and around the arms, legs, and the head.

Follow the drawings to sketch your bear.

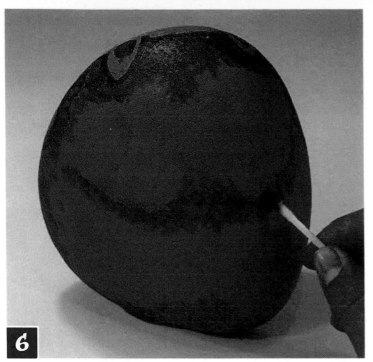

6

Paint the back

Turn the rock over and dab soft shadows at the bottom. Dab wing-shaped shoulder blades just above the center. Also add some shadows behind the ears.

7

Add fuzzy highlights

Mix a tiny dot of your bear's main color with a drop of white paint. Use a clean, damp cotton swab or paintbrush to dot this color around the ears, the top of the head, the tops of the arms, and the tops of the legs.

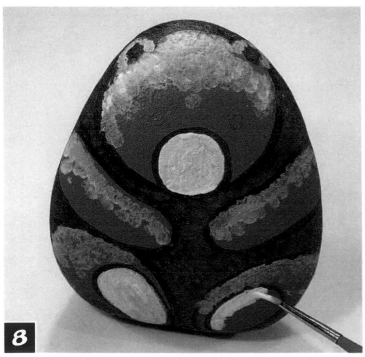

8

Paint the muzzle and feet

Use a small or medium brush and plain white paint to paint the muzzle and the bottoms of the feet.

9

Add black touches

Use your small brush and black paint to darken the shadows around the bottom edge of the head, the bottom edges of the front feet, and between the legs. Then paint two small eyes, a small round nose, and two curved mouth lines below the nose.

Paint the toes

Use black paint to add three small toe lines to each foot. If you like your bear, go to step 13, or you can follow the next steps to add furry details.

Add fur (optional)

To make your bear look furry, add a little water to the color you used in step 7. Use your smallest brush to add tiny lines around the head, ears, legs, and the tops and bottoms of the arms. Add these lines to the shadows on the back of the bear, too.

Add furry shadows (optional)

Rinse your brush and add a little water to the dark color you used in step 4. Make clusters of short brown lines on the bear's cheeks. Also add a row of lines along the bottoms of the arms and legs.

Paint eye highlight

A tiny dot of pure white off center in each black eye will make your bear seem to be looking back at you!

more ideas

bookend bears

Tiny bears make great gifts or party favors. Doll-size straw hats from a craft store come in different sizes to fit almost any rock bear.

heart rocks

> "Rocks come in so many shapes and sizes. It's easier than you might think to find rocks shaped like hearts; long hearts, short hearts, tilted ones, thicker ones, perfect, and not-so-perfect ones. Hearts are a symbol of love, and not just for Valentine's Day!"

No two of these heart-shaped rocks are the same, but each one will look like a heart when it's painted.

Paint a Graduated Color Heart

This is a design that's simple to make. The rock I chose was light in color to begin with, so no undercoat was needed. But most of the time, a white undercoat (or yellow under red paint) will give the rock an extra pop of color.

A light undercoat helps make colors brighter.

Paint the heart's edges

Mix bright red paint with just enough black paint to get a deep maroon color to cover the sides and top edge of the rock. Paint the sides from the bottom all the way up to just inside the top.

Use this deep color to emphasize the heart's pointy bottom and curvy top.

Add a deep red band

Switch to dark red paint to add a narrow band inside the maroon outline.

Add a lighter red band

For the next color band, add enough white paint to get a lighter cherry red color.

Add a pink band

Add more white paint to get a softer pink for the next band. Keep the heart shape distinct as you add these colors.

Add a pale pink band

Add even more white to get this very pale pink shade. Do you see how the heart shape changes with each band you paint?

Add a purple band

Use a liner brush and purple paint to create the outline for the center most heart shape.

Add a gold center

Metallic gold paint gives a touch of "bling." Leaving a narrow outline of plain rock around it helps it stand out.

There are numerous ways to paint heart-shaped rocks. The ones you create may be simple or fancy ones, heart rocks with names or with a message to someone you love. The possibilities are endless!

Here are a few other ways to paint hearts. Can you think of more?

more ideas

Teal, red, pink, and silver gives this heart a rich look.

This heart is done in graduated tones of blue with a silver center. Adding white dots is another option.

This one reminds me of an iced cookie!

This one looks like a hard candy!

Instead of graduated colors, this one is painted in rainbow colors.

Purple and metallic gold is a striking combination.

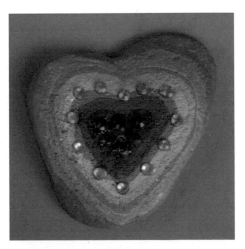

Glue on "jewels" for a different look.

feathered friends

" Do you have a favorite kind of bird? I like them all! Some birds are easier to paint on rocks than others. Here are some of my favorites: Penguins are super easy because the design is so simple. Owls are easy, too, but have more details. Parrots are the most colorful. All these birds can be painted on similar shapes of rock, but parrot rocks should also be taller and a little more tapered or pointy at the top. Baby penguins should be shorter and rounder. "

For most birds, rocks need have a flat bottom to stand up, with rounded or tapering tops.

Pencil

Paint (White and Black)

Small- and Medium-Sized Brushes

Pudgy Penguins

66 Baby penguins are so cute! All you need to paint them are two colors: black and white. Baby penguins are short and sort of round, so it's easy to find rocks to paint. The rock I picked tilts slightly to one side, which is perfect! 99

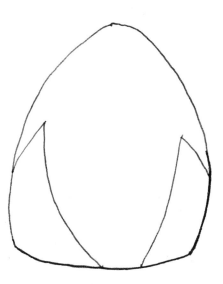

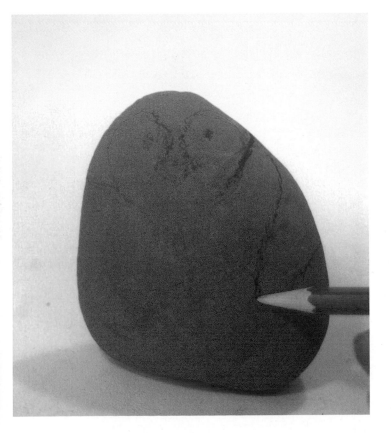

1

Draw on the Design

Draw a circle for the head that occupies most of the top front area of your rock. Dot on two eyes, then draw half-circles above the tops of the eyes that meet in the center of the face, as shown, then curve out to form the beak. Give the bottom of the beak a V-shape. On either side of the head circle, curve a line out a short way then drop down to draw wings that slant outward toward the center of the rock to form a tapering tip. Extend the bottom wing line back toward the side of the rock as shown. On the back side, draw lines from the lower side of each wing, slanting the lines until they meet at the bottom of the rock as a pointed tail. Two small "M" shapes create the feet at the bottom in front.

If your rock is very dark, an undercoat of white paint will make your pencil markings stand out better.

2

Paint white face

If needed, apply two coats to make the white brighter. Make the edges as smooth and as even as you can.

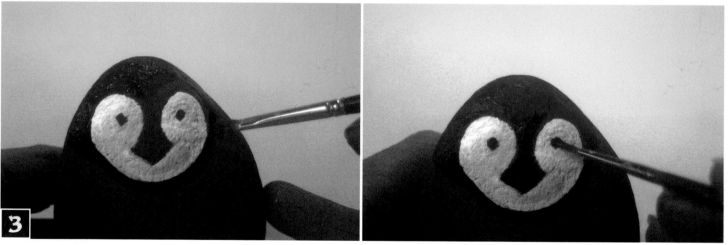

3

Paint black head and beak

Use black paint to go around the shape of the face. Paint the top back of the head all the way down to the tapering back tail. Switch to a smaller brush, if needed, to paint the narrow space between the eyes that goes on to form the beak below. Dot on two black eyes with the handle of your small brush (or use the end of the handle).

4

5

6

Paint the chest and sides

Mix black and white paint to get medium gray and cover the chest and around the wings front and back

Highlight the beak

A narrow gray line highlights to the top half of the beak shape to help it stand out.

Add finishing touches

Finish by using your small brush and black paint to make two small feet at bottom front of the rock. Now your penguin is done!

Pencil

Paint (White, Golden Yellow (Not Metallic), Deep Brown, Bright Yellow, Bright Orange, and Black)

Paint Markers for Details (Optional)

Easy Owls

" Owls are perfect for rock painting. Their compact shape and big eyes make them easy to make. Whooo likes owls? I do! "

1

Find a rock

Look for a rock that stands up without falling over, or use air-dry clay to level the bottom if it's wobbly. Paint a white undercoat and let it dry. Darker rocks may need two coats.

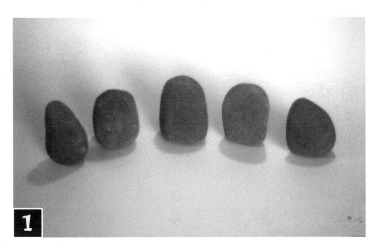

Draw the eyes and beak as shown, then draw the top of the face as a wide half-circle over each eye, with the two ends joining in the center above the beak. The rounded bottom of the face also forms the top of the wings on either side and extends around to form the back of the head. Add slanting wings that frame the owl's chest like curtains, with the wing tips angling back. Turn the rock bring the back edge of each wing straight up to end on either side of the head. On the back side, make a wide U shape that forms the owl's tail feathers. Draw two small feet at the bottom in front as shown.

PAINTING TIP

You can use a hair dryer to help paint dry faster.

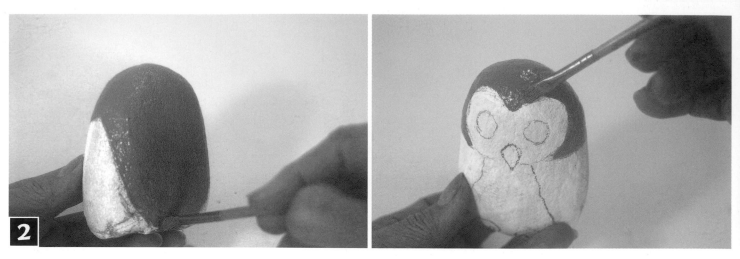

Paint the back side and head

Use a golden yellow color to paint the top of the head, to the edges of the face, and the back down to the bottom of the rock.

Paint dark wings

Any color can be used, but a darker shade makes a nice contrast. Dark brown is a realistic choice.

Fill in beak and feet

Use a small brush and bright orange paint for these features.

Paint eye color

Keep the eye edges smooth and round.

Paint feathers on the back

Use dark brown paint and a rounded brush to paint feather shapes on the back side, starting with a row just below where the head meets the back. Paint the next, slightly larger set, below the first, slanting them in from either side, but decrease the tilt of the two center feathers so that they are straighter than the outer two feathers (on either side). The number of feather shapes you make depends on your brush size and the size of your rock. On mine, I made five feathers along the top and four in the center. At the bottom, I slanted a larger feather shape on either side.

7 Paint feather shapes on wings

Fit oval feather shapes into the shape of the wing as shown.

Note: The edges of the feathers should not touch or overlap.

Add little brown details

You can use a liner brush or brown paint marker to add details that will give your owl more texture. Use a liner brush to outline the eye shapes with dark brown to make them stand out. Outline the beak and feet, and the shape of the face. Next, add a slightly curving, fine line down the center of each gold wing feather. Then, make a fringe of tiny lines below the beak. Along the sides and top of the head, draw or paint short little lines that radiate out and back, following the shape of the head. Finally, on the back side, use a row of tiny lines to define where the head meets the back.

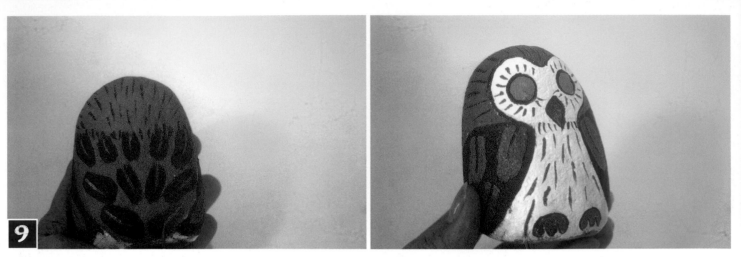

Add little golden yellow details

Rinse your brush and switch to golden yellow paint (or a yellow paint marker) to add curving center veins to the brown feathers on the back. Let dry. On the face, paint little gold lines that radiate out from around each eye. Cover the chest with some short randomly spaced lines starting below the neck and filling the space down to the feet as shown.

Paint the pupils

Use black paint or a paint marker to make matching pupils in the center of each eye.

Finishing touches

Use the pointed handle of a liner brush, a white paint marker, or a very small brush to add a series of tiny dots all the way around the shape of the face outline. Then, place a white dot next to the pupil in each eye to give them their "sparkle."

Choose different color combinations to create more realistic or fanciful looks.

74

Pencil

Paint (White, Bright Red, Bright Yellow, Bright Green, Bright Blue, and Black)

Perky Parrots

❝ There are so many beautiful parrots. It was hard to pick just one to paint, but all the bright colors attracted me to this one. To help the colors "pop," paint a white undercoat first. ❞

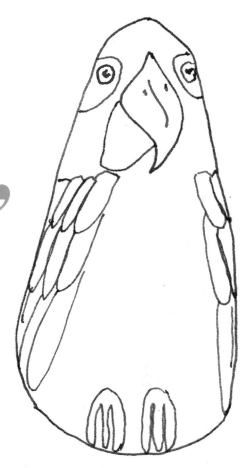

1 Draw on the design

Depending on how tall your rock stands, the head should take up between one-third and one-fourth of the height. I drew the hooked beak first, with a pointed top touching the forehead near the top of the head. Use the pattern as a guide to draw on the rest of the features and feather placement. Place an eye on either side of the upper beak. Draw a jagged or scalloped line around the back of the head and two long slanting feathered wings on either side. On the back the two wings should meet in the middle near the bottom. Below the head, draw the first short set of feathers for yellow wing color, starting on one shoulder.

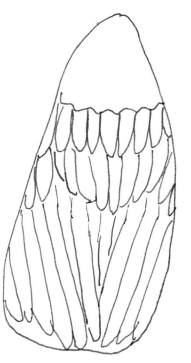

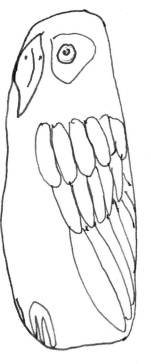

Curve around to the back side, then drop down to form a rounded "apron" shape in the center of the back, before going back up to match the first shoulder. Make a second set directly below for the green feathers on both wings. The last set of wing feathers are the longer blue ones that go the rest of the way to the bottom of the rock. On the back they overlap the matching tail feathers. Each band of wing feathers should have five to six narrow, oval-shaped feathers, and the tips at the bottom of each set should overlap the ones below.

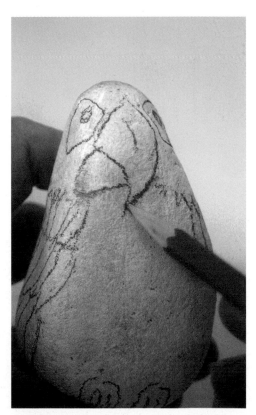

Draw two clawed feet at the bottom of the rock in front, and your parrot is ready to paint.

2 Paint the red areas

Use bright red paint to cover the back and front of the parrot's head, leaving only the beak and eye patches unpainted. Move on to paint the parrot's chest, leaving just the feet unpainted for now.

3 Paint yellow places

On the wings, the bottom tips of the feathers should be rounded. On the back, the yellow patch dips down like an apron. Make the bottom edge slightly jagged or scalloped.

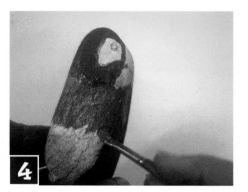

4 Paint green feathers

As with the yellow wing tips, give the lower edge of these green feathers rounded tips that slant just slightly towards the back on either side.

5 Paint blue feathers

For the last set of feathers, use a bright blue paint, and fill the parrot's back with this color. Give the top of the blue feathers a jagged look.

6 Paint the eyes

Use yellow paint to fill in the small eye circles.

7 Add feather details

Use the patterns to help make your feathers look realistic.

Since the blue feathers are already rather dark, add enough white to make a lighter shade of blue, and use it to add create a soft stroke of highlighting down the center of each feather for definition.

Use blue paint to detail the green feathers by outlining the individual feather shapes.

For the yellow feathers, mix yellow with a touch of red to get orange, and use the tip of your brush to outline each feather on the wings.

Outline all yellow feathers across the back and onto the other side.

8 Finishing the parrot's face Add details to the parrot's face.

Use black paint to fill in the bottom half of the beak.

Encircle each eye with narrow black outlines, then give the centers of each eye a small black dot. Add two small dots for nostrils as shown.

9

Paint the feet

Use the same deep gray to paint three gray "toes" like long narrow M's, letting edges of the white base coat show to separate the toes.

Use black paint to outline around the upper beak. Mix black and white paint to get a deep gray, and use this to add a curving line parallel to the outer curve of the beak. This helps make the beak look narrow along the top.

Switch to white paint to highlight the edge of the beak to make it stand out, and brighten the line where the upper and lower beak meet. Touch up the cheek patches, if needed, then add a tiny "sparkle" of white to each eye.

Check your parrot over to make sure it looks finished.

Now you know how to make a whole flock of feathered friends!

rocky reptiles

" Lots of people think frogs, turtles, and even snakes make good pets. My mom said, "No way!" I said, "No problem." I knew I could make my own awesome pet rocks. Here's how I did it. "

Pencil

Paint (Bright Yellow, Lime Green, Medium Green, Orange, Black, and White)

Glitter Paint (Gold, Silver, or Multi-Color) Optional

Fabulous Frogs

" Oval-shaped rocks, or rocks with flattened pear shapes, make great frogs. Look at frog pictures and you'll be amazed by how many different kinds and colors of frogs there are. Lime green ones are my favorite. "

Any of these rock shapes would make a good frog.

This rock is a good size and shape for a frog.

1 Paint the undercoat

Paint the entire rock, even the bottom, with yellow paint. Let dry.

PAINTING TIP

You can use a hair dryer to help paint dry faster.

Paint green basecoat

Use lime green paint to cover the entire top and the sides of the rock, leaving only the bottom yellow. You can make your own lime green by adding small amounts of medium (grass) green paint to yellow paint until you get a color you like. Let your frog rock dry.

Draw the design

If one end of your rock is more tapered than the other, choose the smaller end for the head. Use the pattern in the illustration as a guide to draw on the design.

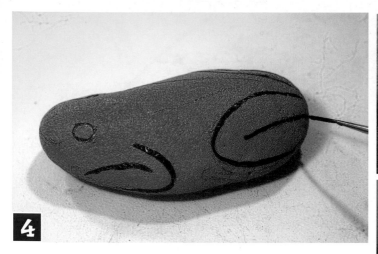

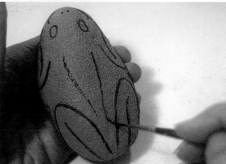

If your lines are not smooth, mix a little more water into your paint, just enough to help the paint glide on. Make sure your eyes are the same size. It's better if they look too big rather than too small. If you don't like the way the face looks, use a damp paper towel to wipe the wet paint away and try again.

Twin lines along either side of the spine give the back some definition.

4

Go over outlines with dark green paint

Mix medium green paint with just enough black to get a very dark green and use a liner brush to go over all the outlines you just drew on.

5

Fill in toes

On my frog, some of the front and back toes are underneath the rock in the yellow areas. Make sure you outline all the toes to make them stand out. You can also fill in with green paint where needed, or wait and paint the toes orange.

6

Other areas to highlight are curved "eyelids" above the eyes, and along the top and bottom of the mouth line. Use a smaller brush if needed. You can also use your finger tip to rub in any paint that needs more blending.

Paint on highlights

Adding highlights helps your frog look more real. Use a soft yellow color and a small round or flat brush with stiff bristles to pick up some paint, then wipe away most of the paint on newspaper, so that you have to "scrub" the remaining paint on. This makes the highlights look softly blended. The main areas to highlight are along the top of the back, the head between the eyes, and along the top curves of the front and back legs, (both the upper legs and the top of the parts folded below). Avoid going over any outlines.

Fill in the eyes and paint the toes

This kind of frog has orange eyes and toes. Use a small brush to paint in the eyes, being careful to keep them even and round. Paint right up to the dark outlines. Then fill in the toes from the round tips to where the toes join the feet.

Paint pupils in eyes and add nostrils

Use black paint and a small brush to give each eye a round pupil in the center. Two small dots between the eyes form the frog's nostrils.

Paint gleams in the eyes

A dot of white paint placed on the edge of the pupil in each eye gives them a wet gleam.

Add some shine

Have you ever noticed how frog skin can look slick? Use gold, silver, or multi-colored glitter paint to add a touch of shine. Brush on glitter along the top and on either side of the two lines down the back, but avoid going over the outlines. Add shimmer to the forehead and along the top curves of the front and back legs. It only takes a little bit to do the job. Glitter paint looks white when wet, but after it's dry, all you will see is some sparkle.

Choose different color combinations and designs to create several kinds of frogs.

Rocky Box Turtle

❝ Did you ever pick up a box turtle and watch it close its shell? I guess that's why they call them box turtles. These turtles usually have plain brown or tan shells, but some have pretty markings on their shell. Here's how I painted mine. ❞

1

Choose a rock

The best rocks for turtles are round or slightly oval, very smooth, and symmetrical (which means the same on both sides). Box turtle shells are more rounded on top while water turtles are usually flatter, so look for rocks that are shaped like a fat hamburger bun.

This is the one I chose.

Paint a basecoat

If your rock is light in color, you may not need an undercoat. My rock is not dark, but I think the paint looks smoother if I cover the rock with an undercoat. I used a sunflower (soft golden shade) yellow to paint all but the very bottom.

Draw on the design

Start by outlining the shell shape with a pencil so it covers almost all the top surface of the rock. It will be oval or round, depending on your rock, but indent the end above where the head will be. Draw an oval head shape, leaving a bit of space between it and the shell. The eyes should be far apart, with the nostrils set in between them. Your turtle's mouth should have a little pointy angle in the center as shown on page 83. Draw the side sections that hold the top of the shell to the turtle's flat bottom shell on either side as shown. The legs are simple oval shapes tilting slightly downward. Make a little triangle of a tail between the back legs. Add a narrow line around the rock just above the bottom to indicate the width of the bottom shell.

Use paint or a paint marker to go over outlines

You can use a liner brush and black paint or a black paint marker to go over your pencil lines to make them stand out.

Fill in the voids

Black paint can make rock seem to disappear! Use a small brush to fill in the space around the head shape, then use a medium size brush to paint the areas surrounding the legs and tail. Don't paint the shell connections between top and bottom shell. If you make a mistake, wipe away wet paint or let the paint dry, and just redo it. Along the bottom of the rock, leave a narrow line of the basecoat color showing as the bottom of the shell.

Paint the shell

Your shell can be any color you like, even purple! But a medium brown color is more realistic. Use a medium or large brush to quickly cover the entire shape of the shell, but leave a narrow band of the golden yellow basecoat showing around the edge.

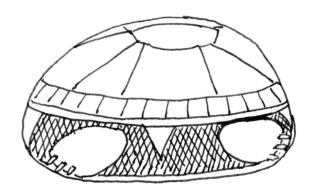

7 Draw or paint the pattern on the shell

When the brown paint has dried, use a pencil to draw guidelines for the shell pattern. Draw a sort of square shape in the center, with curving-out edges on the sides and curving-in edges front and back. Draw a square towards the front of the shell and another in back, then fill in both sides of the shell with three more somewhat square or wedge-shaped sections that are more or less the same size. You can practice on a piece of paper to help figure out how to do this.

When you like the way the shell looks, use a liner brush and black paint, or a black paint marker, to go over the lines.

Finish the shell pattern by filling in the outside border of the shell with short lines all the way around.

8 Paint the turtle's face

After outlining the facial features, add an eyelid shape above each eye, using a liner brush and black paint or a black paint marker to make them.

85

9 Fill in the eyes and paint the shell markings

Dab orange paint inside the black circle shapes of the eyes.

Use orange paint and a liner or other small brush to add lines to each segment of the shell. I put three lines in all of them except for the two smallest segments. There put two. For the center segment, paint a little starburst shape of shorter lines. Make sure all your lines stand out. If needed, go over them with a second coat.

10 Paint pupils in each eye

Pupils can be oval or round but make them the same size and shape in both eyes.

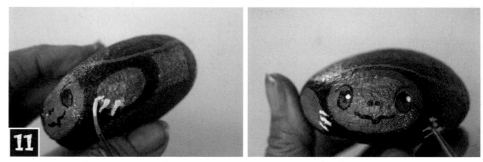

11 Finishing touches

Use white paint and your liner brush to give each foot three little toenails. Dot on a sparkle in each eye.

Here are some of my turtle rocks. My mom liked my turtle so much I made one for her, too!

This was an unusual rock. With practice, you can add even more realistic details!

Stony Snakes

" Some people don't like snakes, but I do. Most snakes aren't poisonous and they just want to be left alone, but others make great pets. Like frogs, there are tons of different snakes. You can try to paint a particular kind, or just make up your own design like I did. "

1

Choose a rock

Almost any smooth, round or oval rock will work. Snake rocks can be more rounded on top or a little flatter, but they should always have a flat bottom.

2

Paint an undercoat and basecoat

Unless you are planning to paint a dark colored snake, cover the rock surface with a light-colored undercoat and let it dry. For this snake, I used a bright lemon yellow color to cover the rock all the way down to the bottom edge.

3 Draw on the coiled snake design

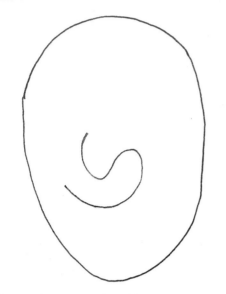

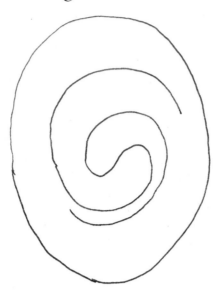

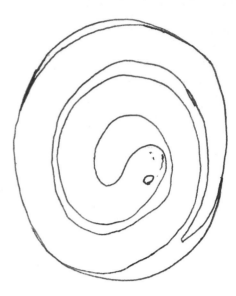

Use a sharp pencil and begin by making the oval shape of the head slightly below the center of your rock. I made the head pointing to the right, but your snake can face in either direction.

Extend a line from the top of the head to form a neck, then turn it in a half-circle around the head shape and stop just below it. From the bottom of the head, draw another line that is parallel to the first line with the distance in between about as wide as a finger. Continue curving that line around until it is right below where the first line ended under the head.

From there, extend both lines around to form another coil, leaving a gap between it and the first coil to separate them. Vary the size of the spaces between your coils for a more natural look. On my snake there was room for two coils because I made the second one thicker until bringing it back around to the front. There I made the bottom line of the coil slant up in the direction of the head and brought the upper line down so that the two tapered to a point to form the tip of the tail.

Paint the snake's spiral shape

When you are happy with how your snake looks, use black paint and a liner brush or a black paint marker to go over the design. Make your lines as smooth as you can.

Fill in around the coils

You can "erase" rock by painting it black. Use a small brush and black paint to fill in the narrow spaces between the snake's coils. Switch to a larger brush to fill in larger areas. Be sure to paint all of the rock below the bottom coil all the way around.

Draw a stripe pattern

Snakes can have all kinds of patterns, but stripes are easy and help add the illusion of roundness to the coils. Use a pencil to make two curved lines just behind the head. Curving the lines makes the snake look round. Skip a space then make another set, a little farther apart. Keep working around the snake's coils making the segments bigger until you are halfway around, then start to make the lines closer together until they are smaller and very close at the tail.

PAINTING TIP

Always start with a damp brush and add a drop of water to the paint for smoother lines.

Paint the segments

I used a deep orange for my snake's stripe color. Outline each segment first then go back and fill them in. Start behind the head and leave a space between each one. Can you see how the curving stripes make the snake look like it has more shape?

Add highlights

To make your snake look more realistic and contoured, add lighter color highlights to the top sides of the coils. Mix pale yellow paint by adding white to the basecoat yellow color. Paint a line just below the top of each of the yellow segments. Switch to bright yellow to highlight the orange segments. As the coils go around, the top side becomes the bottom side, so be careful to highlight only the upper areas of coils when they change directions. Add a line of highlights along the top of the head, as well.

Paint on facial features

Make two small nostrils, using black paint and a liner brush or black paint marker. Add one or two eye circles. Big eyes will give your snake a more cartoon look. Small eyes are more realistic.

Add red details

Fill in the eye circles with red paint, and add a smile line. Add a narrow line of red to the curved end of each orange stripe.

Finishing touches

Give the eye (or eyes if you paint two) a black pupil and when the paint is dry, use the tip of your brush or the tip of the handle to add a tiny white gleam along the side of the pupil.

The snakes you paint can be inspired by nature, or by your imagination.

rock-a-bundle

babies

" My aunt and uncle just had twins! They live far away so I only got to see pictures, but I decided to paint two little babies together on a rock and wrap them up in painted blankets. Real babies don't stay little for long, but these Rock-a-Babies will! And the are fun to make! Here's how to do it. "

Pencil

White Paint for Undercoat

Flesh Tone Paint

Blanket Paint Color of Your Choice (I Used Green)

Brown Paint or a Brown Paint Marker with a Fine Tip

1 Choose a rock

Look for small elongated oval rock. It can be slightly wider at one end. Baby rocks should not be too flat, but have a bottom flat enough so that the rock doesn't roll. Any of the rocks shown here will work as baby rocks.

2 Paint an undercoat

Once you have a rock, paint the entire top, sides, and bottom with a white undercoat of paint.

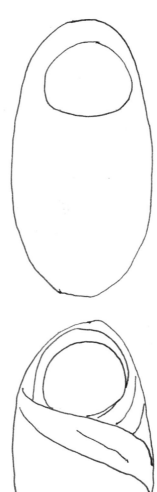

Draw on the design

Even if you don't think you draw very well yet, this is easy to do. Make a round or oval (sideways) head shape near one end of the rock, leaving enough space above the head for the cap or bonnet. Draw a brim around the top and sides of the head covering as shown. Then draw on a blanket that is wrapped snuggly around. Start at one shoulder and make a line that goes diagonally across the baby's chest. Make more lines below the first one, curving them so that they appear to be folds wrapping around the tummy and legs. On the other shoulder, make a few short lines that end at the first fold line, as if tucked underneath.

Paint the baby's head

Pick a color for your baby's skin. I used a color called fleshtone, but you can mix a little red into more white paint and a touch of yellow to make your own. You can add brown or more yellow or red to make whatever skin color you would like your baby to have. Fill in the head oval.

Paint the cap

The cap might be a bonnet or even one end of the blanket wrap. Leave a little strip of white showing around the edge to frame the face, just painting the top and sides. The cap could also be a different color than the blanket, if you like, and the trim can be white or a contrasting color. You could add a bow later if you are painting a girl.

Paint the blanket

What color do you want your blanket to be? Boys often have blue, while girls are often wrapped in pink, but pastel shade of green, yellow, turquoise, or orange are all good colors, too. For my twins rock, I made one pink and one blue because they are a boy and girl, but I chose green for this rock. If you don't have a pastel color, just add white to any color until it is a softer shade.

Use a small flat or round brush to stroke on the diagonal pattern of folds, and leave some narrow lines unpainted so that white undercoat shows through, as I did. Paint the other shoulder, too, where the blanket is tucked. Paint to the bottom of the rock all the way around.

Highlight the folds

Add more white paint to your blanket color to make it a clearly lighter shade, and use this to paint just a few more diagonal highlights without covering up too much of the white showing through. If you make too many highlights, use a liner brush and the original green color to add some diagonal shadows back on between the folds.

Add your baby's features

Use a fine-tipped brown paint marker or a liner brush to give your baby a face. Make wide, U-shaped sleeping eyes spaced far apart in the center between forehead and chin. The nose can be just a tiny dash, and the mouth a line curving at both ends. You can also add a fringe of hair peeking out from under the cap in any color paint you wish.

If you want to paint the folded brim of the cap a different color, do that now. If you like white, you may want to do a second coat of paint. When the paint is dry, you can add a bow, or make stripes or polka dots on the cap if you wish.

Use pale blue or off-white paint for the blanket and metallic gold to add a halo instead of a brim to paint "Baby Jesus" on a rock.

Made for my new cousins, Hazel and Owen!

There are even more fun ways to paint baby rocks, include painting babies in footie pajamas, or painting a Baby Jesus with a halo.

rockin' emojis

Small flat "skipping" rocks make great emojis to paint. Make these to share and trade with your friends or to hide for others to find. Anyone can paint them and everybody loves them. Here's how to do it.

Pencil

Paint (White, School-Bus Yellow, Red, Black)

Assorted round, flat rocks just waiting to be turned into emojis!

1 Paint an undercoat

Cover the top and sides of your rock with a coat of white paint. Let dry.

2 Paint the basecoat

Use bright yellow-orange to cover the undercoat.

Draw the design

Use a pencil to draw on the simple Emoji face.

Paint on outlines

A liner brush and black paint or a fine-tip black paint marker will make the design stand out.

Fill in the mouth

Use dark brown paint (or darken medium brown with a little black paint) to fill in the mouth. Some emojis use black instead of dark brown. Either color is okay.

Fill in the eyes

Fill in the heart-shaped eyes with red paint. Add depth to the eyes by adding a dark brown shadow along the upper left side of each eye.

Here are just a few of the emojis I made to trade and give away.

artsy rocks

"Even though most of the projects in this book are painted to look like animals, birds, or other objects, ordinary rocks can be the "canvas" for making all kinds of artistic designs. Here are some of my favorite ideas."

Paint (White, Aqua, Turquoise, Medium Blue, and Darker Blue)

Small Stiff Brush

Glowing Rocks

" It's pretty cool is to make a rock look like it has a glowing center. Start with a smooth rock about the size of your palm. These were painted on round or oval rocks, but any shape with a fairly smooth surface will work. "

1 Decide on colors and fill in center

The center can be a white or soft yellow glow depending on your other colors. I used white in the center because I'm blending in shades of blue. A yellow center would turn my blue paint green. Choose the colors you want to use and have them ready, because blending the colors together at the edges while they are wet is what makes the rock "glow."

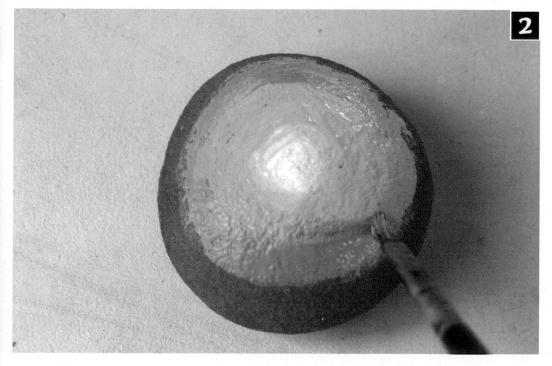

2 Paint the first ring of graduated color

Add a tiny amount of aqua blue to white paint and rub it in a circle just outside the white center. Pick up more aqua without rinsing your brush and make another circle, rubbing the edges so they blend.

Blend in blue shades

When two-thirds of the top surface is covered, pick up a different, deeper shade of blue with your brush without rinsing off the turquoise. Blend this color into the next circle. Keep adding this blue to your brush as you make another blended circle. Then begin picking up your darkest blue. Blend it into the edges of the last circle and paint the remaining rock.

Paint around underside of rock

Use the lid from a jar to hold your rock upside down while you paint the around the bottom of the rock. No plain rock should be seen when the rock is displayed.

5 Design variations and options

For the silver and blue glow rock, I dipped a damp thread into a small puddle of metallic silver paint then lightly dropped and dragged the thread slightly before picking it up and dropping it down on another place, to get this random, frilly looking design. You might have to dip the thread in paint more than once to have enough to cover your rock. For the red rock, I used the tip of my brush handle and white paint to create a dotted pattern.

Sparkle paint gives the green glow rock a bit of dazzle. Use yellow paint for the center. The orange rock also started with a yellow glow, with shades of orange blended in. If you wish, add a starburst of brown dots that are bigger towards the center and then get smaller.

Gold and black art rocks

Turn ordinary rocks into "treasure" rocks by painting them with gold metallic paint, then adding designs with a black paint marker or liner brush.

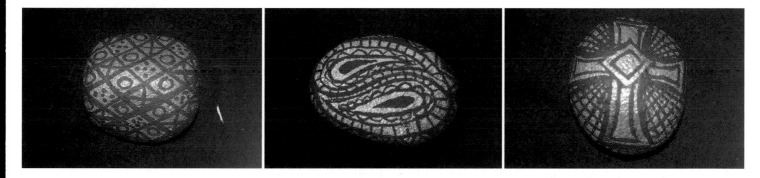

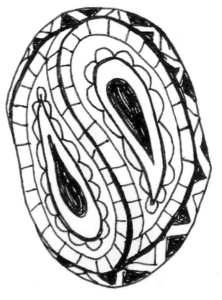

101

Rubber band rocks

Paint a rock any solid color you like, and let it dry. Use rubber bands stretched across the rock in a grid or crisscross pattern to cover up the paint below. The bands can be different widths or all the same. Use small sponge or a stiff paint brush to stipple on a contrasting color of paint so that some of the basecoat still shows through (stippling means to use the bristles of the brush to speckle the surface instead of wiping the paint on). You can add more than one color of stippled paint, but leave some of the original color showing, too. When the paint has dried, remove the rubber band. The effect is sort of like tie-dye.

Sharpie marker decorated rocks

Sharpie markers come in loads of colors and can be used to make tons of fun artsy rocks. A plain rock should be painted with a light-colored basecoat first, so that the marker colors stand out. Sharpies and other permanent markers will bleed through paint that is placed on top of them. However, if they are the top layer, the colors will be bright. Markers may be easier for some kids to use than a brush. The ink in these markers will not wash out, so be careful to cover your work surface and not mark on your clothes.

My parents brought this rock home from a trip they took. The person who did it left the plain rock showing in the center and made a painted frame around the edges.

Paint a sail boat by looking for a rock with a shape that reminds you of a sail, or use any shape or size of rock as a blank "canvas" and paint a sailboat on the sea.

There is not a right or a wrong way to paint on rocks. The designs you can make are limited only by your own imagination. Sometimes the shape of a rock may inspire you. Other times, you might think of something you want to try painting and then look for a rock with a shape that will fit the design. Or you can use the rock as a blank canvas for a scene. You will learn a little more about making art with every rock you paint.

Also Available

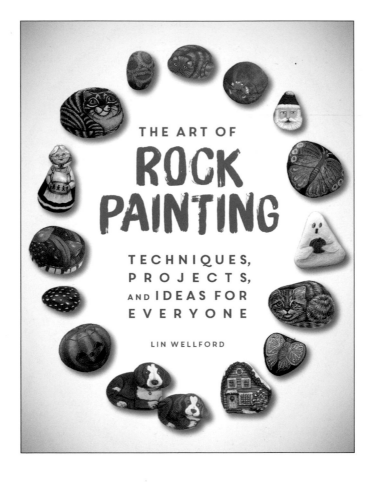

THE ART OF
ROCK PAINTING

TECHNIQUES, PROJECTS, AND IDEAS FOR EVERYONE

LIN WELLFORD